EARTH SCIENCE—OUR PLANET | **Need to Know**

Weather

by D. R. Faust

Consultant: Jordan Stoleru, Science Educator

Minneapolis, Minnesota

Credits

Cover and title page, © John Sirlin/Alamy Stock Photo; 3, © desertsolitaire/Adobe Stock; 5, © Tetiana Soares/iStock; 7A, © Shrinidhi Acharya/Shutterstock; 7B, © studio23/Shutterstock; 7C, © whiran/Shutterstock; 7D, © Saso Novoselic/iStock; 9, © Beautiful landscape/Shutterstock; 11, © stock_shoppe/iStock; 13TL, © Paolo Graziosi/iStock; 13TR, © Feelindesign/Shutterstock; 13BL, © Ed Connor/Shutterstock; 13BR, © S.Borisov/Shutterstock; 15, © Siberian Art/Shutterstock; 17, © Radzas2008/Shutterstock; 19, © LedyX/Shutterstock; 20–21, © John D Sirlin/Shutterstock; 23, © Pau Buera/Shutterstock; 25, © BEST-BACKGROUNDS/Shutterstock; 26, © APFootage/Alamy Stock Photo; 27, © Jayantibhai Movaliya/iStock; 28, © BlueRingMedia/Shutterstock.

Bearport Publishing Company Product Development Team

Publisher: Jen Jenson; Director of Product Development: Spencer Brinker; Editorial Director: Allison Juda; Editor: Cole Nelson; Editor: Tiana Tran; Production Editor: Naomi Reich; Art Director: Kim Jones; Designer: Kayla Eggert; Designer: Steve Scheluchin; Production Specialist: Owen Hamlin

Statement on Usage of Generative Artificial Intelligence

Bearport Publishing remains committed to publishing high-quality nonfiction books. Therefore, we restrict the use of generative AI to ensure accuracy of all text and visual components pertaining to a book's subject. See BearportPublishing.com for details.

Library of Congress Cataloging-in-Publication Data is available at www.loc.gov or upon request from the publisher.

ISBN: 979-8-89577-072-6 (hardcover)
ISBN: 979-8-89577-519-6 (paperback)
ISBN: 979-8-89577-189-1 (ebook)

Copyright © 2026 Bearport Publishing Company. All rights reserved. No part of this publication may be reproduced in whole or in part, stored in any retrieval system, or transmitted in any form or by any means, electronic, mechanical, photocopying, recording, or otherwise, without written permission from the publisher. Bearport Publishing is a division of FlutterBee Education Group.

For more information, write to Bearport Publishing, 3500 American Blvd W, Suite 150, Bloomington, MN 55431.

Contents

Outside Your Window. 4

All About the Atmosphere. 6

The Reasons for the Seasons 10

Wet Weather. 14

Blown Away. 16

Warm and Cold Fronts. 20

Deadly Weather. 22

Bigger Storms 26

How Thunderstorms Form. 28

SilverTips for Success 29

Glossary 30

Read More 31

Learn More Online 31

Index .32

About the Author. 32

Outside Your Window

The weather affects us every day. On rainy days, we may stay inside. On sunny days, we wear sunscreen to protect our skin. But why does the weather change? Understanding the reasons can help us stay prepared.

Earth isn't the only planet with weather. In fact, some planets in our solar system have large storms. The Great Red Spot on Jupiter is a giant storm that has lasted more than 100 years!

All About the Atmosphere

Weather on Earth is shaped by the **atmosphere**. This layer of gases surrounding the planet makes life possible. Energy from the sun travels to our planet in the form of light and heat. The atmosphere traps some of that heat, keeping the temperature on Earth fairly steady.

Weather is what is happening in a place at any given time. **Climate** is the weather patterns over many years.

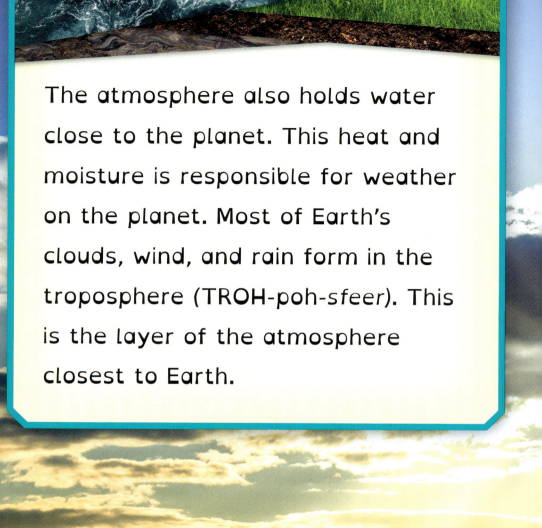

The atmosphere also holds water close to the planet. This heat and moisture is responsible for weather on the planet. Most of Earth's clouds, wind, and rain form in the troposphere (TROH-poh-*sfeer*). This is the layer of the atmosphere closest to Earth.

We measure weather in many different ways. Temperature is how hot or cold the air is. The amount of water in the air is the **humidity**.

The Reasons for the Seasons

The weather in many places changes with the seasons. But what causes the seasons? Earth travels around the sun on a tilted **axis**. This is an imaginary line running through the poles. It angles Earth so part of the planet is tipped more toward the sun.

The **equator** is an imaginary line about halfway between the north and south poles. This region gets about the same amount of sun all year. Most of the time, it is warm.

The part of the planet tipped toward the sun gets more light. This makes the warmer seasons. The part tipped away is in colder winter. As Earth travels through space, the part tilted toward the sun changes. With this change, the seasons shift.

It takes about 365 days for Earth to travel around the sun. Over the stretch of this year, we cycle through all of the seasons.

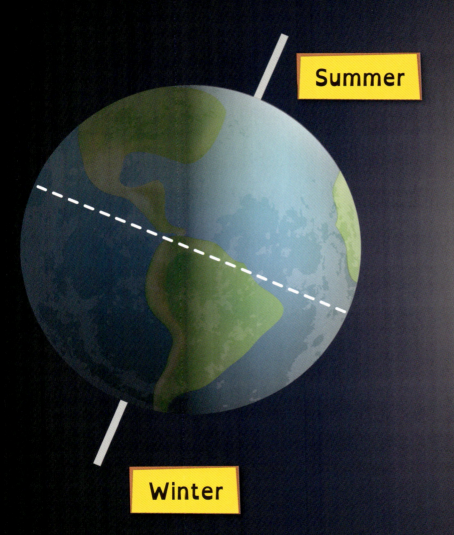

Wet Weather

Water moves around the planet in the **water cycle**. This includes forms of **precipitation**. The cycle starts when sun heats water on Earth's surface. The water rises as a gas called water **vapor**. It gathers to form clouds. Eventually, it falls to the ground as rain, snow, or sleet.

Water is constantly moving through the water cycle. However, very little is moving at once. Most of it is stored in oceans, lakes, clouds, and ice.

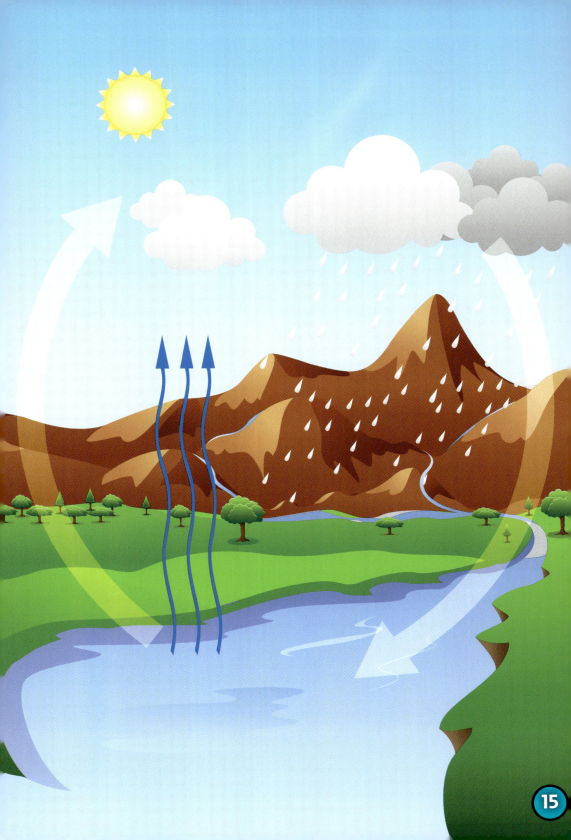

Blown Away

Wind is formed by warm and cold air in the atmosphere. Big blocks of this air move in masses. Warm air masses are lighter than cold ones. So, warm air tends to rise. A cold air mass moves in to fill that space. We feel this moving air as wind.

Air masses can form over land or the ocean. An air mass over the ocean will have more humidity than one that forms above land.

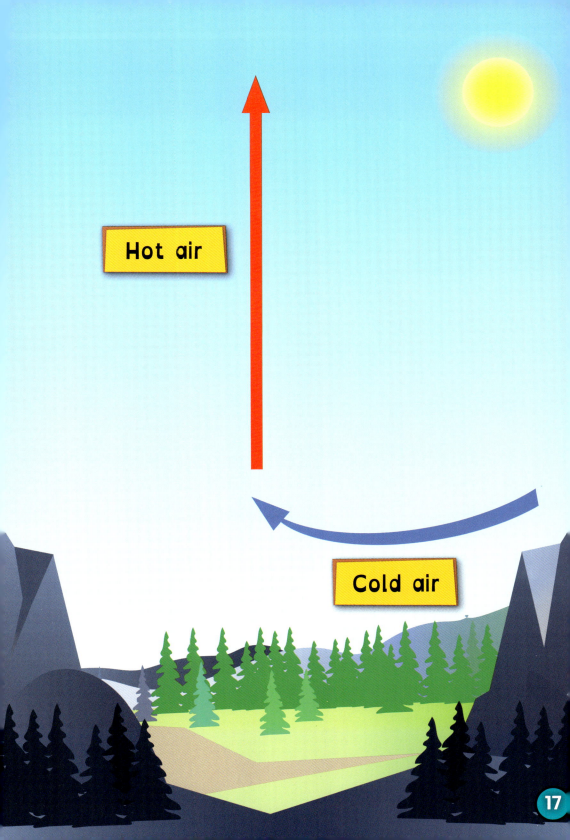

Wind helps move other forms of weather around the planet. It carries heat away from the equator. Rain clouds are also moved by winds. This allows places far from the ocean to get water. Winds can also be strong enough to move solid objects, such as seeds or even sailing ships.

The warm air near the equator tends to travel in winds that move west. These winds are called trade winds. They were used by early sailors to cross the ocean.

Warm and Cold Fronts

Storms often form along fronts. These are places where air masses meet. A warm front occurs when a warm air mass moves into cold air. A cold front is the opposite. Warm fronts tend to move slowly and create high clouds. Cold fronts move quickly, bringing in strong winds and stormy weather.

A cold front moving in can generate a lot of energy. Water droplets in rain clouds rub together to make electricity. Sometimes, this energy is released as lightning.

Deadly Weather

Dangerous storms sometimes form along fronts. Thunderstorms can build up in these areas. They can have heavy rains that may cause floods. Strong winds and lightning are other threats from these storms. In extreme cases, thunderstorms can be deadly.

Warm weather moving in fronts can be dangerous, too. Heat waves are long stretches of warmer than average weather. They can easily turn deadly. Heat waves kill more people than any other weather every year.

Hurricanes are some of the most powerful storms on Earth. They form over the oceans. The warm, humid air there rises quickly. This creates heavy precipitation and strong winds. Hurricane winds can uproot trees and even pick up cars.

These types of storms have different names around the world. In the western Pacific Ocean, they are called typhoons. The storms are called cyclones when they form in the Indian Ocean.

Hurricanes have winds that move at least 74 miles per hour (119 kph).

Bigger Storms

Weather has a big impact on our lives. And Earth's climate is changing. Global temperatures are rising every year. This has led to more heat waves. It has also created stronger storms. Scientists are tracking this changing weather to keep us all safe.

New technologies help scientists study weather. Heavy-duty planes even fly through hurricanes to learn more about them. This helps scientists make predictions about future storms.

Heat waves are happening more often and lasting longer.

How Thunderstorms Form

Thunderstorms bring heavy rain, strong winds, and lightning. Some thunderstorms even have hail. These severe storms often form along a cold front.

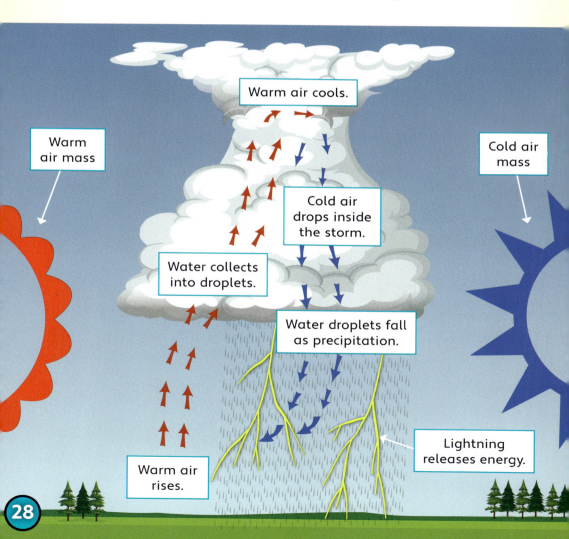

SilverTips for SUCCESS

★ SilverTips for REVIEW

Review what you've learned. Use the text to help you.

Define key terms

air masses
atmosphere
precipitation
thunderstorms
water cycle

Check for understanding

What causes the seasons on Earth?

Explain how winds form.

What can happen when warm and cold air masses meet?

Think deeper

Weather on Earth is changing. How will this affect your life on Earth?

★ SilverTips on TEST-TAKING

- **Make a study plan.** Ask your teacher what the test is going to cover. Then, set aside time to study a little bit every day.

- **Read all the questions carefully.** Be sure you know what is being asked.

- **Skip any questions** you don't know how to answer right away. Mark them and come back later if you have time.

Glossary

atmosphere the layers of gases that surround Earth

axis an imaginary line through a planet or moon, around which the object rotates

climate patterns of weather over a long period of time

equator the imaginary line halfway between the North and South Poles that runs around the middle of Earth

humidity the amount of water in the air

precipitation water that falls to the ground as rain, snow, or hail

vapor water in gas form

water cycle the movement of water around Earth

Read More

Collins, Ailynn. *Hurricanes and the Environment (Disasters and the Environment).* North Mankato, MN: Capstone Press, 2025.

Harasymiw, Martin. *Meteorology (A Look at Earth Science).* New York: Gareth Stevens, 2025.

Wargula, Doris. *Forecasting the Weather (Discover More! A Look at Weather and Climate).* Buffalo, NY: Britannica Educational Publishing, 2025.

Learn More Online

1. Go to **FactSurfer.com** or scan the QR code below.

2. Enter "**Weather**" into the search box.

3. Click on the cover of this book to see a list of websites.

Index

air masses 16, 20, 28

atmosphere 6, 8, 10

clouds 8, 10, 18, 20–21, 28

cyclones 24

front 20–22, 28

heat wave 22, 27

hurricanes 24, 26

precipitation 14, 24, 28

seasons 12, 14

temperature 6, 9, 16, 26

thunderstorms 22, 28

typhoons 24

water cycle 10

wind 8, 10, 16, 18, 20, 22, 24, 26, 28

About the Author

D. R. Faust is a freelance writer of fiction and nonfiction. They live in Queens, NY.